The Painted Sailor

Alyson Hunter

Zenith Publishing

© Alyson Hunter 2005

All Rights Reserved

No part of this publication may be reproduced, stored in a retrieval system, or transmitted, in any form or by any means, electronic, mechanical, photocopying, recording or otherwise without the prior written permission of the publisher.

Disclaimer: The thoughts expressed and images drawn in this book are those of the poet and not necessarily those of the publisher.

National Library of New Zealand Cataloguing-in-Publication Data

Hunter, Alyson, 1948-
The painted sailor.
ISBN 1-877365-06-8
1. Title.
NZ821.3—dc22

First printed in 2005 by Zenith Publishing

Cover *Alyson Hunter at Bassett Road*, 1967
Original photograph by Darcy Lange
Design and typesetting by Angela Gnyp

ZENITH
PUBLISHING

Zenith Publishing
PO Box 752
49-55 Rimu Street extn
New Plymouth
New Zealand
www.zenithpublishing.co.nz

The Painted Sailor

About The Author

Alyson Hunter was born in New Zealand in 1948 and studied Fine Arts at Auckland University before leaving for London to study at Chelsea College of Art and the Royal College of Art.

As a director of Islington Studios and the Islington Graphics Gallery with her husband Hugh Stoneman, she promoted the use of photography in printmaking and her photo-etchings were bought by many public and private collectors. In the 1980s she travelled to New Zealand, Australia and North America, lecturing on printmaking and drawing. Her daughter, Amy, was born in New Zealand in 1981.

Alyson was Master Printer at the Printmaking Workshop, New York and Visiting Professor at the University of Davis, California, 1981 and 1983. Back in London, her writing was published in British anthologies of stories such as *Seeing in the Dark* by Serpent's Tale Press, 1990. With her art, she moved into pure photography, with projects such as the landscape of Thomas Hardy, London Underground and the changing face of Soho. Her portraits of fellow photographers, Dan Farson and Harry Diamond, are in the collection of the National Portrait Gallery, London.

Alyson Hunter lives in North London with her daughter, Amy Frost, a gallery manager.

Acknowledgements

To Colin McCahon for creating in me as a child the unshakable belief in the power of art, and to James K. Baxter for showing me that poetry can speak out in an uncomfortable world.

To Laurie Lee for his support for my poetry in the 1970s, and to Shaun Treacy who first exhibited my poems upstairs in the Queen's Elm.

To my daughter, Amy Frost, who has always believed in me and proved to me I could write anything if kept on the straight and narrow.

To John Rety, my neighbour, for making me laugh about poetry; to Ruth Needham, as my agent in the 1980s, and to Colonel J. J. M. Smail of the *New Zealand News* for sponsoring my poetry at New Zealand House in 1987.

To Lord Blyth for always introducing me as a New Zealander; to Paul Bentley of *The Spectator* for believing in my stories, and to Jay Landesman for telling me in The Groucho, it was about time I published my poetry.

To Michael Horovitz for saying I had a voice; to Simon Usher for my website; to my twin sister, Alexis Hunter, for her unstinting support for my writing; to Paul Ryan for the introduction, and to Raewynne Stonnell and everybody from Zenith Publishing who helped shape this book and get it to the reader.

Contents

About the Author	iv
Acknowledgements	v
List of Images	x-xi
Introduction	xiii-xvii

1960s

Atkinson Road	1
The Wishing Trees	4
Pretty Little School	5
Islander Boy	7
Sweet Factory	8
Army Cadet	9
Whitewash	10
Eclipse of the Moon	11
Young Sharks	12
The Painted Sailor	13
White Horses	15
Azaleas	16
French Bay	17
Grafton Gully	18
Wasp	20
Titirangi	21

Images

    New Zealand 1950s and 1960s   22-38

1970s

To New Zealand Men	39
Pukekura Park	40
Dear Compatriots	41
Karangahape Road	42
A Sense of Place	43
Colonial Farmer	44
Titirangi Revisited	46
Cornwallis Beach	47

1980s

Visiting Hometown	48
Glebe and Capri	51
Balmain	52
Earthquake in New Zealand	53
Nowhere	54
Bendethera Jail	55

Images

    Britain, Spain, Australia, the U.S.A.
    and New Zealand 1970s–2000s   56-72

1990s-2000s

Homeland	73
Worm Farm	75
Displaced	76
Going Back	78
Malcolm	80
Catch the Ferry	82
Library	83
Park Road	84
Piha	85
Air Miles	87
Birthday Party	88
Kopaki Haoari	89
Warrior Tribes	90
White Cliffs	91
Camden Girl	92
Oh London	93
Container	94
Black Sand	96
Asia	97
Made in New Zealand	98

Glossary   99-101

LIST OF IMAGES

pg *New Zealand 1950s and 1960s*

23 *Alyson eating Minties, with her mother Joan, on the section in Atkinson Road, 1950.*

24 *Alexis and Alyson in Titirangi, 1951.*

25 *Alyson on a sleeping donkey, Huia Beach, 1951.*

26 *The Australian grandparents visit New Zealand, 1954.*

27 *Alyson and Alexis with lifetime art subjects – Alyson with bars, men and text, and Alexis with creatures and women, Titirangi, 1957.*

28 *Lyric writing with guitar, 1962.*

29 *Canoeing on Lake Waikaremoana, 1962.*

30 *In Sweetacres Factory canteen with sisters, Alexis and Linley, 1963.*

Sweetacres Factory, Avondale, 1963.

31 *Auckland Girls' Grammar, sixth form art class, 1965.*

32 *Formal Dinner, Auckland University, 1965.*

33 *Students at Elam School of Fine Arts, Auckland University, 1966.*

34 *Alyson and other art students, with tutor Colin McCahon, Grafton Road, 1968.*

35 *In Grafton Road painting studio with self portraits, 1968.*

36 *On patio, Shortland Street, Auckland, 1968.*

Shortland Street house, Auckland, 1968.

37 *30 Park Road, Auckland, 1969.*

Studio, 30 Park Road with poem by James K. Baxter on wall, 1969.

38 *Photograph for exhibition* Some New Painters, *1969.* (Alison Cavell)

pg *Britain, Spain, Australia, the U.S.A. and New Zealand 1970s to 2000s*

57 *Alyson in Evelyn Gardens, Chelsea, London, 1970.*

58 *Photo-etching* Window 71, *1971.*

59 *March for Women's Rights, London, 1973.* (Alyson Hunter)

60 *Darcy playing Flamenco guitar in Moron de la Frontera, 1973.* (Alyson Hunter)

Alyson in Andalusia, 1973, during the dictatorship of Franco. (John Patterson)

61 *Fishermen walking past fish sheds, Newlyn, Cornwall, U.K., 1974.* (Alyson Hunter)

62 *After hours with Islington roofers in the Hen and Chickens, 1976.* (Alyson Hunter)

63 *Formed the Islington Graphics Gallery with her husband, Hugh Stoneman, to exhibit photographic printmaking, 1976.*

64 *Alyson melting aquatint, Islington Studio, 1976.* (Hilda Bernstein)

65 *Adrian and Amy at the hamlet of National Park, Ruapehu, New Zealand, 1981.*

66 *Changing baby's nappy on the way to Hanging Rock, Australia, 1981.*

67 *Photo-etching* Sydney Harbour Bridge, *Australia, 1981.*

68 *Photo-etching* New York, *1981.*

69 *Photo-etching* Across the Tracks, *1983.*

70 *In the French House, Soho, with Dillon and Woodward, 2000.* (Richard Cooke).

71 *Photo-etching* The Colony Room Club, Soho, *1996.*

72 *Alyson's daughter, Amy, back at Piha, New Zealand, 2004.*

Songs of a Double Exile

Introduction

Exiles have two countries – the one in which they live and the one they left behind. The latter is very often the country of the heart, revisited in memory and yearned for in times of solitude. That solitude deepens among those who have something richer and more painful: the double exile that comes from having been born in a country that is not wholly their own, and then leaving it.

Alyson Hunter is a double, perhaps even a triple exile. She was born in New Zealand of Australian-born parents whose own antecedents were English. Her parents chose to leave Australia for New Zealand because they found something culturally lacking in their birthplace. Alyson chose to leave New Zealand for London, the capital of a country her family had long left behind, and a city that once considered itself the governing metropolis of Australasia. Only in London, perhaps, could she confront her own past and the internal landscape of her memories. But what she found there was a crossroads of so many other countries and peoples, and a place whose protean undercurrent drew her down into her own imagination.

Having made her reputation as a visual artist at home (the word 'home' has, of course, an ambiguous meaning for her), Alyson continued on a similar artistic path in

London. Some of her work began to blend the worlds of photography, painting and etching to produce evocations of place. But it was the act of placing herself that became most important, and most difficult for her. From the beginning, her writing was a kind of personal archaeology, a research into feelings and sensations. She plunged into her memory even as she sought to fix the new and changing world around her.

In all of her poems can be found the voice of an outsider, but an outsider who is reaching inside herself and plumbing the society in which she finds herself. The sounds within her poetry are akin to sonar signals: deceptively simple, they bounce back to give information about the proximity and size of things that cannot easily be seen. They map the unseen, emotional space between human beings and their environment.

Some of these poems were composed in New Zealand; others, created in London, revisit memories of a country that the poet has never truly left. Perhaps, in Alyson's childhood and adolescence, New Zealand was a place that called things into question for her. She became acutely conscious of her status as an outsider in the country of her birth; she was, after all, the child of white European migrants. For her, the Maori term pakeha was layered with meaning, and sometimes resonated with an aching tenderness. It signalled that she had been born into exile, but it was much later that she came to realise that it was an exile from which she could never, truly, return.

All that was left, then, was to travel deeper into the state of exile (and that 'state' became her true homeland, one she carried in her mind and her heart). For this reason, London suited her. It is possible to walk its streets and hear accents and languages from a hundred other places but all of them spoken by people who consider themselves 'Londoners'.

Those voices converge, never more so than in the realm of poetry. When you read a poem aloud it is done so in your own voice, but if you are reading it attentively, you will hear something magical. The voice of the poet, personal and touched with a specific, often subtle, accent, can be heard harmonising with your own. Alyson Hunter's poetry has thus become a kind of musical accompaniment to her visual artworks, a counterpoint to the world captured in her eye.

Our senses, as Marcel Proust made plain at great length, can surprise us in the ways that they hold keys to our memories. A sound, a smell, a taste, can hurl us back through time and space with astonishing and dizzying speed and often with more profound effect than might be prompted by a visual reminder. It need hardly be said how swiftly our sense of touch can return us to a vanished moment of intimacy, sometimes with singularly disconcerting effect. Alyson Hunter is alert to these sensual nuances, and her poetry – which is informed throughout by her visual awareness – has allowed her to deepen her response to her world, a world that she recreates and reinvents for all of us.

In the first instant of memory, we begin to construct: we build a framework in which our memories can be properly considered and re-examined. This very act of construction distorts events and sensations from our past, but it is necessary if we are to put them in the kind of order that allows them to return in a way that can be contained and evaluated. At different times, throughout our lives, memories can flood into our minds, often unbidden. They may be very useful, as when the voice of our experience guides us towards or away from a certain course of action; equally, they may be disturbing and difficult to grasp – the haunting presence of a lost love, the dull ache of a long-vanished hurt. Each of us has a personal autobiography being constantly re-written and revised deep within us.

The artist is not necessarily an autobiographer, but memory and sensation are the building blocks of all art. In Alyson Hunter's case, poetry is a kind of autobiography (in the same way as her visual art may be a sort of diary), but it is mediated by her artistry, shaped by her artistry and experience. These poems are a bundle of sensations culled from lived experience. In them we encounter past days of warmth, sunshine and camaraderie, we walk grey London pavements in the slanting rain, and we carry with us, throughout them, the scent of the New Zealand earth that has never left the poet's sensory nerves, and which can be summoned at any time.

The experience of reading them is akin to walking through paintings and stopping a while to study the surroundings, to converse with the characters depicted in them. As we enter these poems, we surrender ourselves to a state of exile – it is a state that many of us fear, but which has the power to enrich us and increase our appreciation of other worlds, other cultures, other times. Alyson Hunter has embraced all of these and made them her own – her work allows us to make them ours.

– PAUL RYAN

Paul Ryan is a writer and broadcaster who has written widely on the arts for a number of international newspapers and magazines and published many books on film and photography. In 1996, he was created Chevalier de l'Ordre des Arts et des Lettres by the French Government.

Atkinson Road

The school milk-shed
is surrounded by poison weed.
Which one smells sweeter?
One suck and you will die.
The fort in the red cliff
Don't ever climb up there
Touch dogs, no never

Now the wishing kauri trees
Don't accept lifts
even from a woman.
Here a wasp nest furious
Throw stones and they will swarm.
See the rich people's drive,
let's creep up it.
Crickets come out with water,
drowning in the clay.
Near lonely Mrs. Thursby
with her Illustrated London News.

The Dutchies have a real Mondrian
of a skeletal house near a skeletal tree
Can we have a look?
They are selling it for the extension.

The brick house, can we play
with the Polio Girl?
No you will make her sad.

The young couple have moved
onto their section
in a caravan. Saving.
Underneath is an ants' nest –
the black ants keep their white eggs
in a black shoe.
Don't bother them
They are in love.

Vast yellow daffodil fields
crushed they have an acrid smell
Don't play in the daffodils
behind Raymond's House.
Polio stricken too

Behind the rubber tree
with its white sap oozing
is an old gum-digger's shed
hidden in the bush
inside, a set of teeth
snarl in a glass above the grate.
No, we never go near the shed.

The bamboo grove
hides the house with a verandah
cool panelled walls within.
Good for spears, bamboo.
No, we were not there.

The woman who lives alone
leads her big black bull
by the nose up the road.
The fathers laugh at her.
Don't ask questions, girlies.

Behind the monkey-apple tree
in a wooden shack
lives an old Maori lady,
the first resident of the road.
She has with her a little blond girl.
Her white face peeps from the window
Shame, adopted,
How will she marry?

Now home at last
the pink drive up to
the white clapboard house
a black Persian cat
surrounded by old lemon trees.
Don't go out again;
Tea is ready.

1962, Titirangi, N.Z.

The Wishing Trees

Sister, do you remember
the two tall kauri trees
close together like twins
near the hot dusty road to home?

Pressing our bodies
between the thick resinous trunks
we wished for speedboats, horses,
America, fame,
and handsome men.

But unsaid
was the wish
to be ugly and weak
and yet
to be singularly
loved.

1962, Titirangi, N.Z.

Pretty Little School

In the pretty little school
the boys dragged him down
the clay bank
and pulled him up again
over and over
his face was bleeding
I did nothing
until I saw a resigned
blankness in his eyes
then I shouted against them
You shouldn't be doing that.

I was called into the classroom
and the muddied boy said
It was her, she was the one
I remember her voice.
I got the strap
and learnt my lesson
in the pretty little school.

The English boy
went into the garden shed
and drank all the weed killer
I saw his grieving parents
they didn't know
he had learnt his lessons well
in the pretty little school.

The brown-haired boy grew up
to be found
bound and headless
in a Thai swamp
he must have missed a lesson
in the pretty little school.

1962, Titirangi, N.Z.

Islander Boy

In the prefab
teacher called up Islander Boy
teacher pulled a knife out
held his arm, scraped his skin
said to our astounded faces
See how dirty you can get.

Islander Boy and I
broke into the Jeweller's house
we lay in all the beds talking
drank Coca Cola from the American icebox
stared at the Manukau Harbour
stretching cold and bleak
outside the vast picture window
and I thought, God how lonely this place is
and I kissed him, as we were eleven.

Islander Boy got in the huge Daimler
I couldn't see him driving,
he was far too small behind the wheel.
The tires crunched on the gravel,
the powerful car moved like a ghost
fast down the fern-ringed drive
and I shouted
Go, Tangi, go!

1962, Titirangi, N.Z.

Sweet Factory

Tortured by this conveyer belt
endlessly moving, inescapable, interminable
the sickly air heavy with hours
I am going mad

My father, handsome and serious
walking around, the boss.
He is bending over a machine

I could touch him
but he might shatter like glass
he would be gone
splintered into fragments.

There might not be
a real man underneath
then I would have no father
just these heavy hours
in this cloying air
alone with this belt
advance, hands, box, retreat.

1962, Avondale, N.Z.

Army Cadet

When the boys talked together
about being at Army Cadet School
they said Waiouru
and then there was a silence
as if a grave had been opened.
Their lips came down on the word
and cut it off.
I was excluded and impressed
they were men now, I thought
they were isolated
it was a man-silence
Waiouru.

1967, Auckland, N.Z.

Whitewash

I went over, just a teenager
and he said
I don't have to talk to you pakeha.
I was taken aback and argued
but the hurt was lying there
he had spoken the truth
I was pakeha, I was white
I was in his land,
there had been a whitewash.

I had thought they always smiled
and had liked us being here.

1969, Wellington, N.Z.

Eclipse of the Moon

In the cold Maori night
the eclipse of the white moon
turns my hand
held face-wards
into black dust,
and silences the furtive spiders
tree-creeping in the ancient stillness.

Dark green-gray stones recall
twisting birth-aches,
and noiselessly the bush-birds
suck in the night-air blankness,
and flitter with open-beaked fear.

Even the blackest beating heart
would be stilled by
this sudden surge of murk
this nefarious
negation of our light
the spirits are about
on this cold old Maori night.

1969, Huia Beach, N.Z.

Young Sharks

The flotsam of war,
their War.
Be grateful for life, they said.
We saw grown men crying quietly.
Their war haunted us too.

So we drifted like sailors,
from a ship blown asunder,
our hearts bobbing in the swell,
floating in the cruel swollen Pacific,
bringing in a new war.

Alone we cried out
to each other, unseen
We are here! Be safe! Peace!

And for a moment there was Paradise,
a dying delusion; salt fever,
as the young sharks took us one by one
and the century darkened again.

Live forever, sharks, take us with you
let us be your flesh
as you break through the water
of a new day
for we were just the baby bastards of war
and peace belongs to you.

1966, Auckland, N.Z.

The Painted Sailor

The Russian sailor
took every stitch off
in the Dean's office
Model, he explained
I see, said the Dean.

I stood behind my easel
in acute shyness
at his panting vulnerability.
The boys giggled behind me
There are no balls in her painting
She doesn't know

I asked a girl
What are they talking about?
she looked at me, shocked,
in complete disbelief
at my innocence.

He stood up
then behind me naked
so close our skin breathed as one
he said softly, Myself and
my ship have been in many ports,
but this painting is the very best
of my Russian soul.

The boys fell silent
safe behind their easels
sailor's salty sweat and oil paint lingered
as we scumbled on.

1966, Auckland, N.Z.

White Horses

Mount Egmont was capped with snow
the herd of white horses
fretted at our smell
and ran wildly around
back and forth in front of the mountain
necks straining, manes flowing.
Beautiful horses.

I have not seen you ride them, I said.
We don't ride them,
we just let them breed,
as they look so beautiful
against our mountain
He replied, smiling.

I felt very City then
and very alone amongst the men,
and felt like running away.
I don't know why.

1967, New Plymouth, N.Z.

Azaleas

His babies, we were just babies
should go to his flower dell
surround the azaleas and rhododendrons
surround them by linking arms
and just stand there,
watching the untended
wither, shrink, and die,
of thirst and unnatural care.
For we are the knowing.
We are the babies,
and we will stand together
strong against him.

1967, New Plymouth, N.Z.

French Bay

I wanted Elvis in a Hawaiian shirt
and sun-spangled guitars
to see yachts
that cut through the swell
with the knife-edged
thrust of money.

But all I had was French Bay
with its sewage and mangrove ripples
I wore plastic sandals wading
for shattered bottles lay unseen.

The man with the brown lips
would buy you an ice-cream
to look up your dress.
Ha ha pervert, you should know
the shop is always closed.

Sandy sandwiches, nothing to drink
shivering in the late summer sun.
All I wanted was
a tiny P-class yacht
to dream on,
and forget
fading French Bay.

1967, Titirangi, N.Z.

Grafton Gully

Young girls suntanned our pigtails jumping
onto Grafton Bridge
baking wide in the Pacific sun.
Nobody has ever walked beneath
and come out the same.
Never survived the sights,
the terrible things that are said to happen,
in Grafton Gully.

I will run through the broken tombs
stepping over the first white people
from Cardiff, Cornwall, Coventry
dead, buried under the soaring concrete span
marching over their colonial dreams.
How I loved this eerie place, this cleft of bush.
Cicadas click and sing, the hum of traffic high above,
the city all around, the beauty of tree and moss.

The moss was under my feet,
the creepers brushed my face
suddenly a dread felt, all too silent,
I turned quickly back
they didn't see me running past
they peered down into the treetops to find me
I met them breathless and they believed.

Excitedly they pressed me for the story
Mellor's voice was mine, the quietness of Clichy
came alive with Miller's Blackest Spring,
and Conrad's blanket tossed young vicars
but they would not go for that,
too high like Grafton bridge
so Zorro tickled a naked woman tied to a tombstone
with a nine-foot feather, and they loved it.

Back in suburbia the telephone rang,
the party line was blocked
by the mother who said,
I had to ask my husband of such vile things
things children shouldn't know.
Grafton Gully was slandered so
her prurient mind writhing pink
and naked on lichen stone
crushing the moss, staring up through lacy frond
pulling creepers down
in her shocked ecstasy.

Mother sent me to Coventry
for a whole month,
and as the silent days grew long and lonely
my heart became a tombstone, hard and broken
secret innocence died as the cicadas sang
undisturbed in Grafton Gully.
Until the developer cleaved the moss
with a sullen motorway.

1967, Auckland, N.Z.

Wasp

Hitching through King Country
three men in the front seat
they are too quiet
thinking woman or child?

A wasp flies into my blouse
and deals a deathly blow
to my beating heart.
Their eyes in the rear view mirror
narrow at my shock
throw me out, don't want the trouble.

To crawl into the cool ditch
with the sweet smell of gorse flowers
the gentle country sounds of
the ticking of a tractor far away
droning out the hours
as I quietly wait for
the happy poison to depart.

1967, King Country, N.Z.

Titirangi

Warm honeyed smell
of yellow gorse
and pink-white tea tree
flowers with ancient
upturned faces.

A paddock downward turning
above, the strong wet smell
of slow cows grazing
on bullock grass
waving in sheets of green.

Silvered jets in the shade
icy water wetly darkens
black and tawny rocks
hiding the deep clear water
beneath

For no man to see
no man to drink
and no man to bathe
and so
break the unseen surface
of Paradise.

1967, Titirangi, N.Z.

New Zealand
1950s and 1960s

*Alyson eating Minties, with her mother Joan,
on the section in Atkinson Road, 1950.*

Alexis and Alyson in Titirangi, 1951.

Alyson on a sleeping donkey, Huia Beach, 1951.

The Australian grandparents visit New Zealand, 1954.

Alyson and Alexis with lifetime art subjects — Alyson with bars, men and text, and Alexis with creatures and women, Titirangi, 1957.

Lyric writing with guitar, 1962.

Canoeing on Lake Waikaremoana, 1962.

In Sweetacres factory canteen with sisters, Alexis and Linley, 1963.

Sweetacres factory, Avondale, 1963.

Auckland Girls' Grammar, sixth form art class, 1965.

Formal Dinner, Auckland University, 1965.

Students at Elam School of Fine Arts, Auckland University, 1966.

Art students (Alyson pictured second from right, sitting), with tutor, Colin McCahon (fourth from right, standing), Grafton Road, 1968.

In Grafton Road painting studio with self portraits, 1968.

On patio, Shortland Street, Auckland, 1968.

Shortland Street house, Auckland, 1968.

30 Park Road, Auckland, 1969.

Studio, 30 Park Road with poem by James K. Baxter on wall, 1969.

Photograph for the exhibition Some New Painters *organised by Alyson at Auckland Society of Arts, 1969.*

To New Zealand Men

Plain men
red carrot faces
bare legs
plastic shoes
cow wives
eat your steak and peas
and drink
your cat's piss beer.

And you
with your non-conformist beard
in your all-angled do-it-yourself
Architectural house
with your
liberated slave-wife
who feeds you
oats and seeds for breakfast
while you dream of
a little piece of land
you can play pioneers on:

The gorse-bush and fern
is growing stronger on the farms
the planes are grounded,
the poisons are banned,
the hills will beat the labour,
and the country will be still again.

1974, New Plymouth, N.Z.

Pukekura Park

Green light filters through the fern
English roses glow softly around us
you ask if we should marry
as the olive creek
moves quietly
over its brown bed.

But no,
it is too late:
the gray Thames
the silver Tamar
the pink stinking rivers of Cadiz
have also moved slowly, ceaselessly
under their still bridges
and now
it is too late.

1974, New Plymouth, N.Z.

Dear Compatriots
(New Zealand House, London)

There you line
ready to feed
struggling against the barrier
your wool clothing
wet from the London rain
steaming.

Bright silly eyes
smug mouths
clutching bags from the airline
truth that you
have been herded from Paris to Rome.

And yet who dares
dislike you
behind fences
in paddocks
clustered fat and white
content, friendly, and generous
eating the grass
that replaces
the dark wet forest
that I have loved.

1974, Haymarket, London, U.K.

Karangahape Road

I went back to Karangahape Road
and walking down
the hot and tawdry street
I saw a crocodile of blue and white schoolgirls
weaving slowly out of the past
dumb, plump, forlorn and untidy.
I searched under the pale panama hats
but I could not find
my green and black eyes
beneath those creamy brims.

Walking past a gutted doorway
I gagged at the memory of London's dark smell
damp grates and rotting clothes,
diesel fumes and spilt beer,
the London of old age betrayed.

But yet, get me back
on a jet-plane
to that old country far away
for my tears for here
are tears for the Englishness
of my blue and white crocodile
and I now belong
to there.

1974, Auckland, N.Z.

A Sense of Place

The big-bellied Comet aeroplane
rose heavily over the green bush.
The woman sitting next to me asked
Is the blue beneath us
lakes and rivers?

I answered
No, they are clouds below us.
Disbelieving, she looked away
so we sat in different spaces

She between earth and clouds
I between clouds and sky

and the aeroplane glistened red
in the late sub-tropical sun
as our shadow moved slowly over
blue, green, brown, yellow
blue, green, blue.

1974, King Country, N.Z.

Colonial Farmer

Your face is creased
with work and pain
as the harsh sun
bakes your skin
into a squint-eyed scowl.
Your thin hair
bred in the cold hard wind
of Skye
no protection in the sweaty heat.

The flies drink
from your scalp.
Brushing them away
your red arm
casts a black banner
of shadow
across your blue eyes
and dry mouth.

The white sun
and coarse brown bracken
will win
and you will walk off
giving not a backward glance
through the man-tears
and heavy country silence
at your broken land.

Knowing
you have worked your blood
into the hard dull clay
and the yellow gorse flowers
and sweet red blackberry
will thrive
having taken their fill.

1974, Urenui, Taranaki, N.Z.

Titirangi Revisited

This uncultured sun
which browns the body
and burns with cancerous stare
lies heavily on tin roofs
and mown lawns.

The thick humid air
carries the silence slowly
checked only
by the domestic whines
of children and machines.

The Waitakere spirits gaze down
through cool pale mists
a darkly frowning green
brooding, still.

The car wheels grate
on the rough metal road
throwing a fine gray dust
onto the silvery leaves around.

Just as the pretentious chatter here
covers in a second
with an irritating cloud
the clear thought
and dulls and cools
a sharp mind's edge.

1975, Titirangi, N.Z.

Cornwallis Beach

But this is not home –
when I touch this salty leaf
cross this sand
see this pier
search these rocks
something is missing.

Home
where the mind stays
the ice wind, the gray sea
malt bittersweet
warm lips on cold glass,
the cliffs and fires
walls and rocks
of England.

English immigrant
now I understand
your look of pain
as each day
and twelve thousand miles
coarsens your mind
and dulls your fear
of these black hills
and quiet white towns
making you
one of us.

1975, Cornwallis, Waitakere, N.Z.

Visiting Hometown

I went back to Hometown
the girls next door
were so sweet, from St. Cuthbert's.
Us girls from Grammar
used to call them St. Custard's
they laughed when I told them.

It was so silly.

Their boyfriends were
in Mount Eden jail
for attacking a car.
The young men trapped inside
were cut open like hibiscus flowers

The sharp machetes.

When the men in the next house
strung high on booze
broke all my windows around me,
berserk, squealing and running
I turned off the lights
so less easy to kill.

Not that I was thinking straight.

Aghast, crouching, I saw
enormous hair
demented shapes
from an old comic book
silhouetted large
on the Hometown walls.

Bottles waving instead of spears.

The woman they caught
scrabbled at my frost-glass door
Don't open it! Don't open it!
Her white palms slid on the blood
red from her melon head
hollow bottles on hollow skull

Those sounds of Hometown.

The teenaged girls
washed my crimson door and steps
because the girls
from St. Custard's
were alright really.
They weren't all that soft.
Or yellow.

The colours of Hometown.

She ended up in the hospital
just around the corner.
The men got to her
so she ran out
with her bandages trailing
behind her down the road.

A vision of Hometown.

Yes, I visited Hometown.

My hometown.

1981, Auckland, N.Z.

Glebe and Capri

The old man from Italy
sits lonely in his house
in Glebe, lonely Glebe.
I asked him, don't you miss

The cypress trees, your wine
the blue sea
deep around Capri
your own blood
singing through the past?

He said, the family is dead.
Nobody to visit there, all dead.
But, I said, there is nobody
here, in Glebe.
I am, he said.

1981, Balmain, Sydney, Australia

Balmain

In the London Inn
we mucked about
played pants-down pool
bet beer on the cricket
dropped acid in the lager
spent all our little money
then put the jukebox on
far too loud.

The old Aborigines
sat apart from us
with their small radio
playing their land's
strange songs
a deep dark pool
of calm and peace.

1981, Balmain, Sydney, Australia

Earthquake in New Zealand

In London
I saw on my television
your green grass shaken apart
and that particular
red earth exposed.

I saw that rain
which grays the distance
and covers all things
with a dull metal gloss
of damp depression.

But I could not feel the wind
that snakes that rain
under my collar
and through my clothes.

That mad driving wet wind
that shouts:

Go home, you Pakeha!
Go back to the old
white world of snowy moors
and black leafless trees.

Go back
For only the red rata blooms
in these bush-clad hills.

1987, London, U.K.

Nowhere

London is for all of us
our safe nowhere land
our Erehwon.

Here the untravelled think
I come from a country
which is all
sheep shaggers
and blackberry bushes.

But Hampstead Heath
is covered in
dogshit and shirtlifters.

And so I might be off
to the country
of six-packs
and the Klu-Klux Klan

Or the home
of the box jellyfish
and the bullshitting barflies.

1987, London, U.K.

Bendethera Jail

My grandmother was born
in Bendethera Jail
to the crack of
the Cat of Nine-tails.
The last time it was used
was in Bendethera Jail.

Within those thick stone walls
his eyes rested from Australia's sun
sat her father, the warder,
thinking
of the cruel clearances
far far away.

His face was set hard
in the hard hot air
sweating it out
in a hard hot country
in a hard, hard time.

2004, Titirangi, N.Z.

*Britain, Spain, Australia, the U.S.A. and New Zealand
1970s–2000s*

Alyson in Evelyn Gardens, Chelsea, London, 1970.

Photo-etching Window 71 *made at Chelsea College of Art, 1971.*
Collection of the Victoria and Albert Museum, London.

March for Women's Rights, London, 1973.

Darcy playing Flamenco guitar in Moron de la Frontera, 1973.

Alyson in Andalusia, 1973, during the dictatorship of Franco.

Fishermen walking past fish sheds, Newlyn, Cornwall, U.K., 1974.

After hours with Islington roofers in the Hen and Chickens, 1976.

*Formed the Islington Graphics Gallery with her husband,
Hugh Stoneman, to exhibit photographic printmaking, 1976.*

Alyson melting aquatint, Islington Studio, 1976.

Adrian and Amy at the hamlet of National Park, Ruapehu, New Zealand, 1981.

Changing baby's nappy on the way to Hanging Rock, Australia, 1981.

Photo-etching Sydney Harbour Bridge, *Australia, 1981.*
Collection of the Gallery of New South Wales.

Photo-etching New York, *1981.*

Photo-etching Across the Tracks, *1983.*
Collection of the University of California.

In the French House, Soho, with Dillon and Woodward, 2000.

Photo-etching The Colony Room Club, Soho, *1996.*

Alyson's daughter, Amy, back at Piha, New Zealand, 2004.

Homeland

This distant sound
becomes a homeland dreamed,
of bush-clad slopes
marching out to the far sea,
there sparkling with Antarctic light.
Land of empty majesty, the clean air
Breath of Heaven itself.

And in the crooks and elbows
small wooden houses crafted white,
hiding the quietest shadows –
those fireplaces, the kauri furniture,
the flies quietly circling inward,
the Southern sun burning through the windowpane,
up along the wallpaper, holding the dust
with the musty Victorian smell of wax and coal
floating where I am not.

The tui singing their searching cadence
up and up, full-throated,
and then the morepork calling in the night.
So still and black, but soft movement there –
the phosphorescence of the sea
licking the black iron-ore sand
with lime-green lip.

Listen to the far-off surf roar,
an ocean coming home.
And listen now, the choked
wet wolf-snarl of London Town.

Drum, drum, together,
both sounds of homeland now.

1997, London, U.K.

Worm Farm

I was getting old, and
he was very old
my Dad.
He said
I will make you breakfast
as he waved his filthy mittens
happily from the garden.

He had been feeding the worms,
a thick pulsating blanket
of writhing pink.
Life at its basest,
rotting circuitous hunger.

A banana I said, don't peel it.
He looked so gleeful
to be feeding me
it broke my heart.

I have some apples here,
For the worms, I said.
He looked at them aghast
They are far too big!
And far too fresh!
He looked at me with anger
and went back to feed
his new unspeakable children.

2000, Titirangi, N.Z.

Displaced

When the country came to town
and hordes of tweed
invaded the empty weekend city
an African stared in disbelief
at the jolly souls.
A smiling white mass
choking Westminster.

But my heart was gripped
seeing a dinosaur
dying in a swamp.

My heart ached, for
Millie-Molly-Mandy might be there
tottering along, old now,
not the girl from England
I read about,
lisping under the fern tree,
the moist muzzle of the cow
nuzzling at my shoulder.

Afterwards, I walked up the Hampstead Road,
and saw people from Somalia, Croatia, and Rwanda,
learning English from glowing white squares
high in the tower blocks.

I felt torn, my ancestral English blood
was calling, you are Country
Come back with us, Country Girl.

Astride my urban street
in bewitching beauty
my night-time friend the fox
pauses, as do I.
We are statues carved in lamplight.
In the silence he tells me
Be calm, be cheerful, it is all right
for London Town
is our countryside now.

2003, London, U.K.

Going Back

Oh, to go back and hear
the fog horns on the ships
at midnight, New Years Eve
so loud, so many, so grand,
in Auckland Harbour.

The children strapped
with a leather strap
on their outstretched hand.
Offenders birched
behind wooden walls.
Homosexuals crying
in Mount Eden jail.
The boys from Dakota and Idaho
fresh faced, arm in arm
loving victory in Vietnam
taking Rest and Recreation
in old Queen Street.
The Maori
in his black shirt and silver fern
kicking a ball around South Africa
proud to be an
Honorary White.

I cannot go back home
as the English there
cannot take the return ship.

Shores left forever, for
I have loved this, their
changing London,
for home is
a country not
peopled by the past.

2003, London, U.K.

Malcolm

Malcolm, like the song sang
I was seventeen and you were eighteen
fragile haughty brother sister prancing in
the big wooden house in Parnell.

It is long gone, gone, with flowers in your hair
the bees can't find the daisies
that grew wild in the grass
when they come back from afar.

I never saw your face again, they told me
You have to forget, why go there,
something about an axe, attempted manslaughter.

I, too, have been at that edge, and fate
she pulled me away, Malcolm.

So you will always be a bright
willow-legged boy in jeans
my handsome genius, as lost as I
amongst our ragged self-esteem
that coiled inside us.

The police caught you even then
you looked a boy amongst men
ashen-faced in Grafton Gully.

I abandoned your friendship
he told me to, a long time ago
It's the right thing to do.

We married the bar-top instead,
loved others less sweet
when I was seventeen and you were eighteen
in the hot dusty days of Parnell.

2003, London, U.K.

Catch the Ferry

Catch the ferry from the Rocks
pass under the bridge
wave to your Great-Uncle
in the tall building close by.
He will not see you
he must be a hundred by now.

Dock at Balmain
Do they still knock the pier?
That good feeling
as the boat shuddered
like a horse under you.

Walk up the main street,
feel my arms holding you
two decades ago.
Perhaps it will be like a dream.

Some small remembrance
of the vast ships
moored to the street
the huge flank so exciting
brute bulk against brute sea.

Me carrying you
of you being a baby
in easy, lucky Sydney.

2004, London, U.K.

Library

My family went to the library
on Friday nights
as if it was a church
words from the whole world
the hush of centuries.

One night outside
Father disarmed a man with a rifle
who was threatening the quiet people.
It was never mentioned again
or we children never heard.

The London literary agent said to me
People who use libraries are bad
they should buy books
borrowing books is bad.

I was as shocked
as if she had pointed a rifle
at my whole family
walking together
each with their own treasured selection
on that dark fern-ringed road
beneath the sparkling stare
of the Milky Way.

One gun, one person,
took the library away from me.

2004, London, U.K.

Park Road

On the back of my hand
you suddenly scarred me
intently, you of the kind
prison pallor, Buddhist,
and the poet was shocked.

Grieving at our parting
I had to forgive you
the silent tattoo, this trace of you
these blind words
I carry still.

Your pallor was destroyed
cindered or earthed I do not know
this mark endures, furious
until I too am gone.

I do remember you
for one of us
was marked down
by the breathless braggart,
one of us was doomed.

2004, Titirangi, N.Z.

Piha

Oh Piha, that Martian beach
with Lion Rock
set square amongst the surf.
That black sand so hot
you had to burrow like a sand flea
to get to your towel.

The caves, the smell so cold and salty
as dense as the fear of drowning.

I walked in my sleep
to the reed-filled lagoon
velvet waters whispered to me
I heard my sister's voice, far behind
she caught me, on the bank,
just in time.

We walked safely back
to the old canvas tent
in the bullock-grass field
with the roar of the waves
spume from Antarctica
flashing in the night.

Linley, can you hear?

The clouds of pink candyfloss
towering in azure air
mountains of sparkling ice
with untouched birds calling.

Do they call to me?
Are they still calling?

Calling me back home.

2004, London, U.K.

Air Miles

Waking up in panic
the weight of the space
to get here
preys on my mind.

The aeroplanes crashed
so few of them really
and New York is another world
I can get away again.

The distance grabs me by the throat
sits on my shoulders
thirteen thousand miles
and yet this is a quaint quiet place
dangling down upon my breast
a pendant of islands
a tiki left in a drawer
with a string
that is too long.

2004, Titirangi, N.Z.

Birthday Party

New Zealand Judiciary
Dame Sian Elias
I am sorry I shook the Coca-Cola bottle
and squirted everybody at your birthday party.

The jelly and ice-cream was heaven
and your Dad had hired a grey donkey
for us to ride
on that sunny sloping lawn.
Your party was so good
I just had to be bad.

2004, Titirangi, N.Z.

Kopaki Haoari

The white man came
he gave you a distrustful God
who said you were Heathen
and took your souls tightly
in his cool white hand.

He brought the sharpest axes,
the rifles and bullets
that killed your most savage enemy.
Pots that never broke
and jewels that sparkled.

He brought you influenza
as dank as the valley,
he bought prostitution
and new laws for himself.
He drove stakes in the land
then said it was his.

He passed his blood into yours
until there was not a man standing.
But you are the mist and the rain
the forest wind hides you
the highest kauri is your pew
and nothing can deny you.

2004, Titirangi, N.Z.

Warrior Tribes

The bloodied Scot lay on the heather
his tartan cloak lay on the ground
the English so strong together
dashed the tribes with sword and leather
into the hills around.

For the Scots did fight each other
tribal enmity did them down.

So when faced with muskets and cloak of feather
the English fought with facts well known
a bloodied Maori lay on the heather.
Tribal enmity did him down.

2004, Titirangi, N.Z.

White Cliffs

White cliffs in North Taranaki
under green undulating fields
so like Dover, this kissed by a new sun
land so familiar
and yet so far away.

In eighteen sixty-nine, she walked
here with her children
on that summer's day
to return home
to Maniapoto warriors
sitting on her armchairs
standing on her rugs
looking through her windows.
Oh Annie, too far away from Dover
on that sunny day.

2004, Titirangi, N.Z.

Camden Girl

Some primitive need
made me come back here
to have you born.

Or was it that the queue was so long
in Whittington Hospital.
The air here is cleaner I suppose
but then there is the rip
up in the ozone.

Now we are back as Kiwis
and you have hired a car
You and your Camden school friend
driving through the rainforest
on Lone Kauri Road.

A safe little cocoon of London
hurtling around the bends.

2004, Waitakere, N.Z.

Oh London

How I miss your great furnace
I was just a green twig
engulfed by you
reforming me, moulding me.

We are the long white cloud
invisible, transient, neutral.
Colonials in your belly
thousands of us, so discreet.

How right I was to leave here
and be a mote forever
rebranded
in your consuming greatness,
dear old London Town.

2004, Titirangi, N.Z.

Container

The radar picks up
submerged containers
thrown from heaving decks
by violent ocean storms.
They rip a hole in passing ships
death awaiting under the waterline.

So sailors radio to the Navies around
Japan, France, Australia, Russia
to come and blow the doors off
and send it bottom bound.

Now Aotearoa has a cargo necklace
Oh no! the seagulls cry

And octopus with his fingers
opens the refrigerator to peep inside
just an empty place
where nothing foody lingers

Fishy darts away from
her dark reflection
in car-mirror, windows open wide
nothing now for her detection

Clam sucks his blue lips
over a hundred telephones
silently, for there are no pips
nobody listening to the moans

And big sharky
squeezes through Venetian blinds
in blue and cream to sell
as they flicker in the swell
breaking them, and nobody minds

A consumer coral ring
of cargo goods deep-down lie
around far off islands.

Oh no! the seagulls cry.

2004, Titirangi, N.Z.

Black Sand

In a dusty city
I longed for your dusky sand
I thought of you
as scorched, hard, as black as soot.

But when upon you again
with the rushing roar of the Tasman Sea
curling in my ear
you were as soft as bath powder
a creamy frothed cappuccino
a caramel confection
falling into my rounded footsteps
sand in a timer
slipping through my fingers.

2004, Karekare, N.Z.

Asia

I walk down Queen Street and see the new people
could I be in Pusan or Nanjing?
Do I sometimes long for a pakeha face
like mine?
The longer I am away
the less pakeha I am.
Travel has made me more understanding,
more rounded, global, less provincial.
Trying to understand.

Am I in the Middle of Nowhere
Or in Asia's vast domain?

I walk now in London's Chinatown
and wave to Tu and Sun
I always feel at home here
perhaps it reminds me of Auckland
a Chinese party long ago
the boys throwing firecrackers
girls smiling shyly
settlers too.

2004, Auckland, N.Z./London, U.K.

Made in New Zealand

I sewed the flag upon my jeans
and smarted at the English jibes
I missed that glaring sun
and Maori singing
had me wipe a tear away.

Back in the superette
I see those words, Raro, Edmonds,
things I always ate
and remember rolling Jaffas in the dark
that noisy picture theatre lark.

I remember
the *Oriana* sailing off
to the blast of steam escaping.
Hearing *Now is the Hour*
from the singing tearful throng
a lonely leaving bower

Soho I live and breathe
but for me
Made in New Zealand
I will always be.

2004, Titirangi, N.Z.

Glossary

Avondale. Suburb of west Auckland.

Balmain. Area of Sydney, Australia reached by ferry.

Bendethera. Old shale mining town in Australia.

bullock grass. Name for rough grass.

Country Alliance. The Countryside Alliance, made up of British farmers and workers who felt their rights were eroded, especially with the banning of fox hunting under PM Blair's Labour Government.

Edmonds. New Zealand brand of baking powder.

Erewhon. Book written by 19th-century English writer, Samuel Butler, based on New Zealand; nowhere spelt backwards (taking into account Butler's treatment of 'wh' as a single letter).

Glebe. An inner-city suburb of Sydney, Australia.

Huia Beach. Found on the edge of the Manukau Harbour, surrounded by the Waitakere Ranges, New Zealand.

Islander. Term in use for emigrants from Pacific Islands such as Tonga and Samoa, who travelled to New Zealand in the 1960s to look for work.

Jaffas. Round, candy coated chocolates.

Karekare. Surf beach, west Auckland, New Zealand.

kauri. Native pine tree of New Zealand.

King Country. Named after Maori chieftains who fought in the Maori Wars. The region is located west of Lake Taupo, New Zealand.

Kopaki Haoari. Maori; covered weapon, usually a club.

Lake Waikaremoana. Situated in Te Urewera National Park, East Coast of the North Island, New Zealand.

Maniapoto (Ngati Maniapoto). A Maori tribe of the King Country.

Manukau Harbour. Situated in south-west Auckland region of New Zealand, opening to the Tasman Sea.

Milly-Molly-Mandy. A toddlers' book printed in Britain before the war, with illustrations of thatched cottages and country gardens. Most literature of that time, of any sort, was written in England and North America and shipped to New Zealand.

morepork. Native New Zealand owl, named after its call at night.

Mount Egmont (Mount Taranaki). Solitary mountain centrally located in Taranaki, New Zealand.

pakeha. Maori term used for white European emigrants to New Zealand.

Pants-down pool. Australian expression in playing pool; if your opponent putts all the balls off the table, ie a whiteout, you have to pull your pants down in front of spectators.

Parnell. Central suburb of Auckland, New Zealand.

Piha. Large surf beach in west Auckland, New Zealand.

poison weed. Plant commonly known as Deadly Nightshade.

prefab. Prefabricated classroom built for the children of the 'baby boom' generation born after WWII.

Pukekura Park. Large 49-hectare park located in central New Plymouth, New Zealand.

rata. Native New Zealand tree bearing red flowers in December.

Raro. Brand of orange juice in 1950s New Zealand.

St. Cuthbert's. Catholic Girls' School in Auckland, New Zealand.

Tasman Sea. Stretch of water between Australia and New Zealand.

tea-tree. Common name used to describe the native New Zealand shrub, Manuka.

The Rocks. Historical part of Sydney Harbour, Australia.

Titirangi. Suburb of west Auckland, New Zealand.

tiki. Maori greenstone pendant, typically of a carved face or figure.

tui. Native New Zealand song bird with a beautiful sound and distinct white chest feathers.

Waiouru. Isolated army cadet camp in the central North Island of New Zealand.

Waitakere [Ranges]. Range of hills, thickly covered with native bush in west Auckland, New Zealand.